Arcadian Ballads

Arcadian Ballads

by James Reeves

with illustrations by

Edward Ardizzone

Heinemann
London

Heinemann Educational Books Ltd
LONDON EDINBURGH MELBOURNE AUCKLAND TORONTO
HONG KONG SINGAPORE KUALA LUMPUR IBADAN
NAIROBI JOHANNESBURG LUSAKA NEW DELHI KINGSTON

First published 1977 in a limited edition by
The Whittington Press

This edition first published 1978

British Library Cataloguing in Publication Data
Reeves, James
Arcadian ballads.
I. Title II. Ardizzone, Edward
III. Ovid. Metamorphoses. *Adaptations.*
821'.9'14 PR6035.E38A

ISBN 0-435-14772-2

Published by Heinemann Educational Books Ltd
48 Charles Street, London W1X 8AH
Printed in Great Britain by
Cox & Wyman Ltd., London, Fakenham,
and Reading

These poems are based on Ovid's *Metamorphoses*, from which they have been very freely adapted. Only the first is not strictly Arcadian, the legend being Babylonian, not Greek.

J.R.

Contents

Pyramus and Thisbe

Trees in distinguished gardens hung with fruit
In curious minds revive a myth.
Ancient against ancient walls they stand,
Centennial boughs sustained by props.
Into a bishop's hand
The blood-dark mouldering harvest drops.
All delicate palates praise this mulberry,
This blood-dark mulberry
Purple as the bishop's jowl
And over-ripe like scholarship.
In prehistoric days the mulberry
Grew, not blood-red, but white,
White as the plumage of a snowy owl.

The Feud

In Babylon, time-foundered city
Long buried in mud and sand,
Lived Pyramus and Thisbe once,
And they walked hand in hand.

Pyramus was the noblest youth
In all that burning land.
Dark Thisbe was the loveliest girl,
And they walked hand in hand.

Hand in hand by day they walked,
By night they kissed and clung.
They kissed and sighed each other's names,
For they were fond and young.

Old and hard their fathers were.
These angry quarrelling men
Ordered their children, boy and girl,
Never to meet again.

'Thisbe, my Thisbe,' Pyramus groaned,
Alone in the cool of night.
'Pyramus, Pyramus,' Thisbe moaned,
'Must love be killed by spite?'

Can love be jailed in walls of brick,
By parents be forbidden?
Its flame will all the hotter burn
Because it must be hidden.

Between their gardens stood a wall,
Scowling and high and thick.
These lovers found a reed-thin crack
Between a brick and a brick.

Through this the lovers spoke their love
In halting desperate fashion;
The longer they were kept apart
The fiercer grew their passion.

They cursed the wall for parting them,
But for the crack they blessed it;
They thanked the wall with tearful joy;
With burning lips they pressed it.

'Thisbe, I cannot live without you;
Without you I shall die,'
So went the whisper through the wall.
'This very night we fly.

This fateful night we fly from home,
Escape our cruel doom.
Meet me at moonrise, Thisbe dear,
By ancient Ninus' tomb.'

Pyramus

The girl in dread, with stealthy tread,
Slid out into the night.
None saw her go: her dress was black,
Her face was veiled from sight.

Below the towers of Babylon
A wandering river flows;
Beside this stream stands Ninus' tomb,
And there a mulberry grows.

The mulberries hang ripe and full
And white as virgin snows.
Here Thisbe came with eager step
And when the moon arose:

'Come quickly, Pyramus,' she breathed,
'I fear to be alone.'
Then suddenly a dreadful thing
Turned her wild heart to stone.

To slake her thirst a lioness
Came loping to the water,
Its bloody paws and drooling jaws
Incarnadined with slaughter.

Poor Thisbe saw the creature's shadow;
Struck dumb and terrified,
She ran to find a cave nearby,
There in the dark to hide.

But as she ran, she dropped her veil.
The lion, dripping gore,
Snatched up the veil with teeth and talons,
Then ripped, and rent, and tore.

When Pyramus reached the tomb, to meet
His love as they had planned,
He saw the paw-prints of the beast
Fresh in the moonlit sand.

And then he saw the bloody veil:
Sheer horror stopped his breath.
'Oh God,' he thought, 'my love is slain,
Gone to a ghastly death.

'She died alone; the shame is mine.
I should have been here first.
Now let me die by my own hand
Where I should live accurst.'

Beside the tomb stood Pyramus,
Beneath the mulberry tree.
He bared his breast, he bared his blade.
'I come, my love,' cried he.

The sword into his valiant heart
He drove with deadly might.
Out rushed his blood. A crimson flood
Engulfed the berries white;

It soaked the earth about the tree
And drenched it to the root.
It stained with its own mournful hue
The clusters of ripe fruit.

Thisbe

Dark Thisbe then with timid step
Came from her sheltering cave;
She longed to clasp the valiant boy
She was too late to save.

She found the tomb beside the stream;
The mulberry tree she found;
And then she saw her lover's form
Writhing upon the ground.

An instant horror gripped her mind,
Made all her body quake.
'Pyramus,' she stammered, 'you are dead.
Is it for Thisbe's sake

'That you are slain, my only love?'
She saw her mangled veil,
The empty scabbard at his side,
And guessed the grisly tale.

She grasped his body, kissed his lips.
'Sweet Pyramus', she cried.
He heard her voice and felt her touch,
Smiled through his tears and died.

'Death shall not part us,' Thisbe sobbed.
'I will not live alone.
This sword that has your sweet life robbed
Shall rob me of my own.'

She drew the blade from Pyramus' breast,
Then on her knees she prayed:
'Almighty Jove, grant that in death
Together we be laid.

'And you, O tree, for ever bear
Fruit of this mournful hue,
That youths and maids in after time
Think of us lovers true.'

Beneath her breast the sword she pressed,
Fell forward on the blade.
Lifeless she lay by Pyramus.
All was as she had prayed:

Too late the cruel fathers wept
Over their children's doom,
Sealed Pyramus' and Thisbe's love
Together in one tomb.

Fathers and lovers now are dust,
And Babylon is dead.
Still grows the ancient mulberry tree,
Its dark fruit overhead.

Remember two whose passionate hearts
Burned with a mutual fire,
Recall the blood together spilled
In anguish and desire.

Pan and Syrinx

A music in the forest sounds
Its plaintive, reedy note,
As if the trembling melody
Came from a lovesick throat.

But it is neither girl nor boy
Nor amorous nightingale,
It is the forest god himself
Of whom I tell the tale.

Syrinx, a woodland nymph, was slim;
Arcadian hill and plain
Knew none more virtuous. She was
Of chaste Diana's train.

None was more swift and sure of foot
Than Syrinx in the chase.
None aimed her bow at buck and doe
With deadlier skill or grace.

Satyrs and spirits of the wood
Pursued the girl in vain,
For to Diana she had vowed
A virgin to remain.

Fast though they were, these ravishers,
When hotfoot they pursued,
Chaste Syrinx, sinuous and wild,
Was faster to elude.

One day as through the woods she strode,
Returning from the chase,
She saw upon the dappled track
A shaggy form and face.

Two short, curled horns sprang from his head
Amidst a crown of spines,
For this was Pan the forest god
And lord among the pines.

What caused the nameless sudden fear
That fell on those who trod
The forest way at close of day?
It was this goatfoot god.

Extreme desire possessed the god.
He raised his hands in prayer.
'Hear me,' said he. 'I never saw
A maiden half so fair.

'O live with me and be my queen;
I cannot live without you.
I burn with eagerness to fold
These two strong arms about you.

'I long to fondle your soft hair
And kiss your matchless face.
Come near, sweet girl, you have no cause
To fear a god's embrace.'

Syrinx was terrified to hear
His wheedling, husky tones.
She felt as if she could not breathe;
A panic locked her bones.

'I cannot love or live with you,'
At last she faintly said.
'Diana is my god. For her
I live and die a maid.'

Nimbly Pan seized her by the wrist.
'No, you are mine,' cried he.
His goatish touch restored her strength,
And Syrinx struggled free.

Now on winged feet she threaded swift
The pathless solitude.
Between the darkening trees she ran;
The goatfoot god pursued.

Huntress and hunter down the hill
Followed their twisting race.
Arcadian woods had never known
So swift, so grim a chase.

Out of the trees, across the plain,
Hunter and huntress tore.
Then in her flight Syrinx was stopped
By Ladon's sandy shore.

The river spirits then she prayed
To help her in her need.
On her in triumph sprang the god
To sate his goatish greed.

The river maidens heard her prayer
And snatched her from his grasp.
'Where has she gone? What have I here?'
Was Pan's frustrated gasp.

For in his arms a tuft of reeds
And not a girl he found.
A tuft of reeds she had become
In Ladon's marshy ground.

As Pan beside the river stood,
Sighing his grief away,
A wind arose and through the reeds
Softly began to play.

A song of love the wind intoned,
Of unappeased desire,
Of passion's fever, aching thirst,
And grey, extinguished fire.

The god, enraptured by the sound,
Cut reeds of varying length,
Fashioned himself a set of pipes
And blew with gentle strength.

The hollow stems obeyed his touch.
A tune of plaintive yearning
Expressed his grief and quenched the love
Within his wild breast burning.

'Lost lovely Syrinx,' Pan besought,
'Come back, come back once more.'
So Pan lamented many days
By Ladon's reedy shore.

A music by the river sounds.
The wavering notes complain.
Among the shades the nymph is fled
And Pan laments in vain.

Echo and Narcissus

Now hear the ancient poet trace
The record of a girl and boy:
The girl the mirror to a voice,
The boy the echo of a face.

Narcissus

Narcissus, loved by boys and girls,
At sixteen was the fairest youth
That mortal eyes had ever seen.
At sixteen he had learned this truth –

The truth that beauty was his curse:
It had been good to be admired
As if his form had been a god's.
It had been good to be desired.

He sought out friends, and in their eyes
His godlike looks Narcissus read.
Their adoration swelled his breast;
Their flattery turned his golden head.

'All are in love with me,' he thought.
'I can have any friend I choose.
Love is a game,' he told himself,
'A game Narcissus cannot lose.'

Yet the vain boy let none come near.
No friend might touch him, none embrace.
At length one lover he had scorned
Called on the gods to make redress.

'Use this proud boy as he used us;
Avenge our pain, wise powers above.
Is it not just that he should feel
The pain of unregarded love?'

Nemesis, God of fate, looked down.
He heard the prayer; his doom was quick.
At once Narcissus hated praise,
And honeyed flattery made him sick.

Startled by silence, and afraid,
Narcissus called 'Is no one here?'
'Here,' answered Echo. 'Where?' cried he,
But Echo only answered 'Where?'

'I die in anguish and despair,'
Narcissus groaned. 'Will none love me?'
'Love me,' was Echo's sad reply.
He heard her now, but could not see.

'How can I love a viewless ghost,
A mocking voice?' Narcissus cried.
She flung herself upon the boy.
He cast her off in scorn and pride.

Crazed by her slighted love, the girl
Haunted the caves and hills alone.
Her youth, her beauty, both are lost.
Body and heart are turned to stone.

When anguished lover calls aloud,
'Oh, is my loved one's heart of stone?'
The voice of Echo from the rocks
Calls back 'Of stone – of stone – of stone.'

Echo

Echo, the pretty chattering girl,
Offended Juno, heaven's queen.
The goddess in her rage ordained
That Echo should no more be seen.

Unbodied ghost, she haunts the woods.
Unseen but seeing, all alone,
Sadly she strays from cliff to cave
And has no word that is her own.

She has no word but yours or mine
Or anyone's that lifts his voice.
And if we curse, then she must curse,
But if we laugh, she must rejoice.

When lover weeps for his lost love
And cries 'Come back or I shall die',
'Shall die - die - die' is all he hears.
The taunt is Echo's sad reply.

Golden Narcissus, now forlorn,
With heart for neither love nor sport,
Loitered about the pastures wild
In frantic unrewarding thought.

Echo beheld him, straight and slim.
Love at first sight possessed her mind.
'Fair boy,' she breathed, 'look on me now -
Look on poor Echo and be kind.'

Narcissus neither saw nor heard,
Each day as by himself he strayed.
His restless steps were followed close
By the unseen and voiceless maid.

Those he had loved he hated now;
Their love for him had loathsome grown,
He could not bear their company
And chose thenceforth to walk alone.

He could not bear their company;
His own he soon began to hate.
Trapped by self-love he had no choice
But to endure his desperate fate.

So at sixteen Narcissus knew
That merciless beauty is a curse,
That to make sport of friends is bad
But to despise yourself is worse.

The Pool

Deep in the unfrequented hills a pool
Of lucid, quiet water
Mirrors the depth of bluest heaven.
Encircling willows make it dark and cool.

Here comes no goat-boy with his strolling herd.
The calm is never broken
By raucous beast or plaint of bird.
Here strays Narcissus in his desolation.

To slake his thirst beside the pool he lies,
His peerless head bent down.
Then such a vision meets his eyes
As seems the end to all his fevered longing.

Entranced he lies and drinks his own reflection,
Perfect in form and feature.
'Never,' he gasps, 'has human creature
Been worthy of my love but this alone.'

Pools in a deeper pool, his eyes bewitch him,
His smile smiles up to him.
It is his capture and his snare,
Caught in the tangles of his flowing hair.

He strains his arms to fondle and embrace
The body in the water.
Day after day in vain despair
He burns to kiss his own infatuate face.

Snared in the mirror of his own perfection,
'Why can we never meet,
Why never touch?' Narcissus mourns.
Only fond hope he meets in his reflection.

For sleep or food Narcissus has no care.
Hourly he wastes away.
Only the stern gods hear him pray:
'Come soon, sweet death - come, sweet and bitter death.'

The Flower

Wildly they mourned Narcissus dead,
The shepherds and the shepherd maids.
Wildly they wept, as slow they bore
His body to the infernal shades.

Even as he crossed the Stygian shore
To that inhospitable place,
He seemed to view his wasted limbs,
The tangled gold, the matchless face.

The water-nymphs lamented him.
'We loved you,' came their passionate cry,
And slighted Echo mourned alone -
'Loved you' was her forgiving sigh.

Now where he suffered by the pool,
A white-encircled flower of gold
Sprang from the earth, slender and straight,
Its drooping head was pale and cold.

This is the flower we name Narcissus.
This image of a chaste dejection
Records the ill-starred boy who died
Enamoured of his own reflection.

Old, blind Tiresias, Ovid tells,
This chronicle was first to trace -
Of Echo, mirror to a voice,
Narcissus echo of a face.

Arachne

Spider, spider, weave your web,
Scuttling, shuttling, low and high;
Cast your airy, cunning net;
Snare the unwary, foolish fly.

Gossamers from bush to bough
In the diamond dews of dawn
Trap the gadfly, mayfly, dayfly
Winging lakeward from the lawn.

Spider, spider, weave your web,
Scuttling, shuttling to and fro.
I will tell how you began
Many hundred years ago.

The Weaver

Arachne was the only child
Of an old dyer and his wife.
They worked obscurely in a cottage,
And simple was their way of life.

One gift the gods had given Arachne.
It was not beauty or high birth.
Yet maids and matrons came to view her
From the four corners of the earth.

Nymphs of Tmolus and of Pactolus
Quitted their reedy fountains chill,
Drawn to the dyer's narrow cottage
By famed Arachne's matchless skill.

It was a rare delight to see
Arachne weave, Arachne spin.
Her dancing wrists were deft and pliant,
Her nimble fingers long and thin.

And as she worked, the watchers sensed
A note of magic in each thread.
They sighed in wonderment and awe:
'Arachne weaves our dreams,' they said.

'It is as if Minerva taught her,
God of the loom divinely skilled.
From her alone the girl has learned.'
But proud Arachne stamped and shrilled:

'Holy Minerva taught me nothing.
She is no cleverer than I.
If she would like a weaving match,
Let her come down from heaven and try.

'If she can beat me at my trade,
She may do what she likes with me.'
Minerva heard the boastful word.
'Presumptuous peasant-girl,' said she.

‘Hear her blaspheme against the gods.
For such a crime she shall atone.’
Straightway she floated down to earth
Transformed into a mumbling crone.

With crutch in hand and bearded chin
She hobbled to Arachne’s side.
‘Let an old woman counsel you:
Forswear my dear the sin of pride.

‘My ears are sharp, I heard you speak.
Repent your words of scorn and pride.
Kneel down and ask the god’s forgiveness - ’
‘Stupid old hag,’ Arachne cried.

‘Save up your breath to cool your porridge.
Minerva, if she knows her trade,
Can have a contest any time.
Perhaps the Great One is afraid.’

Minerva spoke. ‘Not so, young woman.
Behold, the god herself is here.’
She cast away the beard, the crutch.
The onlookers bowed low in fear.

Only Arachne stood unmoved,
Blushing a little for her sin.
Yet still she hoped that in a match
Against the goddess she might win.

‘Obstinate girl,’ the watchers said,
‘To think she can escape her doom.’
No further word Minerva spoke
But silently set up her loom.

The Contest

Arachne wove; Minerva wove.
Their many-coloured spools
Between the threads their dancing fingers threw.
The shuttles flashed like gilded fish in pools,
So fast they flew.

Great silence froze the lookers-on.
They marvelled as they saw
Kingfisher colours, the softly gleaming wool,
The growing webs. With unbelieving awe
Their breasts were full.

All day the goddess and the girl
Handled the glowing threads
Of wine-rich purple, gorgeous peacock hue,
Of misty yellows, iridescent reds,
And purest Tyrian blue.

All day the crowd surveyed the strife.
They saw the shuttles run,
On lengthening webs the lengthening shadows fall.
Tireless and dumb, Arachne worked like one
Who fashioned her own pall.

Minerva's storied tapestry
Of antique glories told.
It pictured Agamemnon's tragic act,
And how Achilles murdered Hector bold
When burning Troy was sacked.

The might of the immortal gods,
The High King's ruling thunder,
Athens, her citadel and special glory,
Of such things all who viewed her web of wonder
Might read the woven story.

Loves of the gods Arachne wove,
Their deeds of guile and shame -
How Jove on Danaë in sunbeams shone,
And to Europa as a white bull came,
To Leda as a swan.

The rape of Proserpine by Pluto,
And Neptune's sorceries
Among the mermaids on the crested billows,
And gods with nymphs beneath the flowering trees
With flowering banks for pillows -

The living world her art revealed,
Live birds in whispering leaves.
The viewers broke into applause at last.
'How like a god,' they cried, 'this mortal weaves!
Her skill is unsurpassed.'

Minerva's Rage

'Enough of this,' Minerva stormed.
'Be silent, all you impious churls.'
Yet in her heart she knew her art
To be no better than the girl's.

Such flawless work in heaven or earth
No eye had ever seen before.
So in her wounded majesty
The jealous goddess raged the more.

Fearful it was to see a goddess
In such high passion stamp and swear.
Still worse to see her grasp the web
And strand by strand its beauty tear.

Arachne's masterpiece she tore,
In screaming fury, thread from thread,
And then she seized a boxwood spindle
And struck the girl about the head.

Arachne's face and head she struck,
And when the royal wrath abated
Arachne, shedding tears of shame,
Was silent and humiliated.

A rope hung from the cottage roof.
The girl, her art, her pride in wreck,
Knotted the rope in desperation
And fixed the noose about her neck.

'Arrogant fool, she shall not die.
Her life I spare,' Minerva said.
'For ever shall this weaver live,
Suspended on her slender thread.'

The goddess spoke and took her leave.
As she withdrew, a spell she spelled,
By which Arachne lost her hair;
Her head grew small, her stomach swelled;

Slim fingers turned to spidery legs.
So up and down her silken rope
The matchless weaver to this day
Travels with neither pride nor hope.

Callisto

Twinkle, Twinkle, Little Bear
Through the clear and frosty air,
Out of space and out of time.
How on earth did you get there?
- That's the subject of this rhyme.

I

As Jove was patrolling the ramparts of heaven
He spied a fair nymph in the valley below.
She slept in the shade of an evergreen glade;
On the ground just beside her was lying her bow.

Her hair was outspread on her pillowing quiver;
Her fingers touched lightly the shaft of a spear,
For the nymph served the huntress, the moon-cold Diana.
To this virgin Callisto no man might come near.

Jove looked on Callisto with swift-mounting passion.
'We will visit,' said he, 'this flower of Arcadia.
Our dear jealous Juno, our wife, shall not see us
As we sport in this grove, for nowhere is shadier.'

So, taking the shape of the goddess of hunting,
He woke up Callisto and spoke in this manner:
'Too long have I missed you, sweet votaress most favoured.
Come close now and welcome your mistress, Diana.'

Less cool was his kiss - so it seemed to Callisto -
Than the usual greeting bestowed by her queen,
Whose embrace grew still fonder as they sat down together
In a spot well concealed by the trees' leafy screen.

'Now let's talk of hunting,' began the deceiver.
'Let's talk of the game, the pursuit and the kill.'
So she told of the chase till the god's fast embrace
She could not resist, and great Jove had his will.

The god had his will and departed from earth.
Callisto had struggled - she was not to blame.
Distracted she fled from the grove of dishonour;
She hated herself and the place of her shame.

At last she went back to her hunting companions.
With the goddess herself she was sad and aloof.
The nymphs saw her blushes and guessed at the reason;
They voiced no suspicion but waited for proof.

The moon waxed and waned, and the time slipped away;
Callisto no longer could hide her disgrace.
How swift in their spite was the train of wise virgins;
How righteous in wrath was the Queen of the Chase.

'Oh wretch!' cried Diana, 'no votaress of mine
Brought ever such shame to this order before.
Such gross impropriety no decent society
Can permit. Now begone - let us see you no more.'

So, betrayed by one god and spurned by another,
Callisto departed, unloved and forlorn
To a far desert place where none knew her disgrace;
And there in due season her baby was born.

II

Meanwhile, back in heaven, abode of the gods,
All talked of Jove's latest adventure on earth.
There was winking and whispering among the immortals
As soon as they heard of the boy Arcas' birth.

Cried Juno, Jove's consort: 'This is really too much.
Beyond all endurance these whispers and winks.'
She flew to Arcadia in search of Callisto,
Determined to punish the beautiful minx.

She found the poor girl with her innocent babe.
With curses and insults she grasped her long hair.
Callisto in vain begged the goddess for mercy,
And was instantly changed to a black, shaggy bear.

She lost her soft voice; it became a harsh growl.
Her lips were transformed into wide-gaping jaws.
Her beauty in ruin, this miserable bruin
With horror perceived that her fingers were claws.

Though converted by Juno to a grisly bruno,
She yet had a heart to feel grief and despair.
Half human, half beast, she roamed the wild places
In fear of her life from the bow and the snare.

III

So passed fifteen years during which her son Arcas
Grew up as an orphan, without an idea
As to who were his parents or where he was born.
He ranged the wild places with hatchet and spear.

Callisto one morning came out of the forest
And saw her own son at the end of the glade.
She knew him at once and stepped forward to greet him,
But her grunt of affection made Arcas afraid.

She spread wide her motherly arms to embrace him.
Her endearments were piteous, and piteous his fright.
As the creature drew near, he brandished his spear,
Then prayed to the gods and made ready to fight.

Jove heard his son's prayer. Said he to himself:
'This has gone far enough. We will now intervene.'
So, arriving in time to stop scandal and crime,
With a flash and a crash he appeared on the scene.

First Arcas his son to a boy-bear he turned;
Then he raised a great whirlwind which carried them high
Above earth, above heaven, to outermost space,
Where as Great Bear and Little Bear they shone in the sky.

Cried Jove: 'That's a glorious fate for Callisto;
An equally glorious end for the boy.
They shall shine as immortals in outermost space;
They shall shine every night to bring wonder and joy.'

Whatever the truth of this singular tale,
There they circle and glitter, these two constellations.
On a clear frosty night you may best view the sight,
A joy and a marvel to all generations.